America's
NATIONAL PARKS

America's
NATIONAL PARKS

ELLEN WINSLOW

GALLERY BOOKS
An Imprint of W.H. Smith Publishers, Inc.
112 Madison Avenue
New York, New York 10016

A FRIEDMAN GROUP BOOK

This edition published in 1991 by GALLERY BOOKS
An imprint of W.H. Smith Publishers, Inc.
112 Madison Avenue
New York, New York 10016

ISBN 0-8317-03563

AMERICA'S NATIONAL PARKS
was prepared and produced by
Michael Friedman Publishing Group, Inc.
15 West 26th Street
New York, NY 10010

Editor: Megumi Yamamoto
Art Director: Jeff Batzli
Designer: Devorah Levinrad
Layout: Helayne Messing
Photography Editor: Christopher Bain

Output by Linographics Corporation
Color separations by Scantrans (Pte.) Ltd.
Printed and bound in Singapore by Tien Wah Press (Pte.) Ltd.

Gallery Books are available for bulk purchase for sales promotions and premium use. For details write or
telephone the Manager of Special Sales, W.H. Smith Publishers, Inc., 112 Madison Avenue,
New York, New York 10016. (212) 532-6600

*To my father, who was a
great help to me.*

Table of Contents

BELOW:
They don't mind a bit if you call them buffalo, but members of the herd in the Hayden Valley would much rather be called bison. It helps take the sting out of the memories of the days of the Wild West. But the valley, with the Yellowstone River meandering through it, stirs vivid memories of those thrilling days of yesteryear when millions of these huge creatures roamed free through the heart of America.

Anyone who visits a national park in the United States or Canada, or anywhere in the world, for that matter, is following in the footsteps of an adventuresome man named John Colter. He was an explorer, a trapper, and in his later years became known around St. Louis as the biggest liar the American West has ever produced. Actually, he was an honest man. But the tales he told of the things he'd seen in the Rocky Mountains were just too incredible to be believed.

He couldn't stop talking about pools of water that were so hot you could boil fish in one, even in the dead of winter. He loved to describe jets of steam rising hundreds of feet in the air, and bubbling cauldrons of mud that produced a noise that sounded like dozens of bullfrogs all grumbling at once. He said he had seen bright red mountains, some that were yellow, and one that appeared to be made of glass. No one ever tired of hearing his yarns, but it's no wonder that no one believed him. The poor man had spent four years alone up there in the mountains, after all, and that's enough to make any one a little dotty.

Jim Bridger spent even more time in that place they called "Colter's Hell," and when he settled down with a trading post on the Oregon Trail, folks passing through in wagon trains considered his yarns a high point of their trip. Of course, no one believed Bridger either. It wasn't until 1869, when the government put together a scientific expedition to see what these old mountain men were talking about, that the truth began to come out. But even scientists didn't quite trust their own experience. This place on the Continental Divide was a combination of the Garden of Eden and the pits of Hell.

But they were willing to give it the benefit of the doubt, and over the following two summers other expeditions went into the wilderness. Near the end of the 1870 exploration, members of the party got to talking around a campfire one night. They all agreed that they were in an incredibly beautiful place, but couldn't help wondering what the future would hold when developers discovered it. Some of them even thought it might be a good idea to stake some claims for themselves. One of them, Cornelius

Hedges, argued that private ownership would destroy the place and came up with a revolutionary idea: What if the government claimed it all and preserved it for the enjoyment and education of all the people? He was very convincing, and before the campfire went out that night, he had the whole party sold on the idea. But they weren't out of the woods by a long shot; they knew they had their work cut out for them. Hedges started the ball rolling with an article in a Montana newspaper, and Nathaniel P. Langford, another member of the party, took the idea on the road with a lecture tour of important Eastern cities, including Washington, D.C. Meanwhile, other members of the expedition convinced the Montana territorial delegate to Congress, William H. Claggett, to introduce a bill calling for the creation of a national park in the vicinity of the Yellowstone River.

It wasn't an easy idea to sell. No one in the world had ever heard of such a thing as a national park, and almost no one in Congress had ever heard of the Yellowstone River. This was remedied by publishing more articles and sending reprints to anyone who might have any influence. They descended as a body on Washington to buttonhole every member of Congress they could reach. Claggett introduced his bill on December 18, 1871; on March 1, 1872, President Ulysses S. Grant signed it into law, making Yellowstone the world's first national park. The idea of setting aside tracts of land for pure pleasure wasn't new. Almost no prince or potentate since the dawn of time had been without a private preserve. But this was the first one set aside for the people. And what a gift it has turned out to be.

Less than 120 years later, there are forty-nine national parks in the United States, and another twenty-nine in Canada.

The first Canadian national park was established in the Rocky Mountains at Banff in 1885. If any old trappers had seen its lakes and ice fields before then, they didn't bother to tell anyone. Credit for its discovery goes to surveyors who found hot springs on the slopes of Sulphur Mountain while mapping a route for the Canadian Pacific Railroad. Almost from the day they were found, commercial interests moved in and began fighting

ABOVE:
One of the overlooks along Trail Ridge Road offers a view across Forest Canyon in Rocky Mountain National Park. A paved pathway there allows closeup looks at the tundra. There are more than 300 miles (483 km) of pathways in the park, including the Five Senses Trail, one of the first anywhere designed for the enjoyment of the handicapped. The park also includes an area known as Handicamp, which allows handicapped visitors to enjoy backcountry camping.

ABOVE:

*Moose are among the memories
nearly every visitor to Banff
takes home. They roam through
most parts of the park and
generally seem oblivious to the
presence of humans. It isn't
uncommon for them to wander
into campsites looking for a
change of pace from their diet of
willow leaves, or to wander into
the middle of roadways. There
are four distinct geological
zones within the park —
mountain, prairie, lowland
forest, and arctic wilderness —
and each supports its own
specialized plant and
animal life.*

among themselves over who had the right to exploit them. The government settled the argument by surrounding them with a park.

The railroad people, who named the place Banff for a county in Scotland, were quick to take advantage of its spectacular location. When the Canadian Pacific's investors were trying to increase support for their venture, they built luxurious rolling stock with extra-large beds, extra-heavy wood paneling, and solid brass fittings inside and out. What it added up to were very heavy trains that couldn't make the trip over the mountains. When the railroad began service, this problem was solved by building a string of hotels along their right-of-way, allowing them to eliminate sleeping cars and cut down the size of their dining cars. The crown jewel of the chain was the Banff Springs Hotel, which, along with its neighbor, Chateau Lake Louise, quickly became more popular as a destination than as a rest-stop. And the new national park became Canada's number one tourist attraction.

Hotels and other visitor services notwithstanding, the central idea behind the creation of national parks is to prevent commercial development and to preserve the natural landscape. In North America, this natural landscape includes the river of grass that is the Everglades and the rivers of ice in northern Canada. It includes deserts and mountain lakes, active volcanoes and peaceful flower-filled valleys, rugged seacoasts and fragile wetlands. In some national parks, the natural landscape is even hostile to visitors. You'll need to hire a small airplane to get you to Auyuittuq National Park, on Canada's Baffin Island, and after that the best route to the heart of the park is by Eskimo canoe up Pagnirtung Fiord, but only after the ice begins to break up in the middle of August. Nahanni National Park, in the Northwest Territories, is also only accessible by small airplane or canoe, and like Auyuittuq, it's nowhere near the beaten path. On the other hand, Pukaskwa National Park on the shore of Lake Superior in Ontario, not far from what we call civilization, can be reached only on foot or by canoe. In contrast, Great Smoky Mountain National Park in Tennessee and North Carolina can be seen almost completely from behind the wheel of your car, which may help to explain why it is the most-visited park in the United States.

Parks Canada, which administers the Canadian national parks, has identified forty-eight separate natural regions, and plans to establish a park in each of them. They have already placed at least one in every province, and though the mountains of Alberta have nine of them, the Canadian parks are evenly distributed from coast to coast. The bulk of the national parks in the United States, on the other hand, are west of the Mississippi River, partly because there was less unspoiled territory in the East when the idea took root. There are eight national parks in Alaska, six in California, and five in Utah.

But the National Park Service administers much more than the forty-nine national parks in the United States. A national park is established by an act of Congress, but there are almost eighty other sites that have been designated "National Monuments" either by Congress or by presidential proclamation. The basic difference between the two designations is most often size. A park usually encompasses a variety of natural features, but a monument can be as small and specific as the Statue of Liberty or Dinosaur National Monument in Colorado or Muir Woods in California. A national monument designation may be the first step toward becoming a national park, as happened in the case of Arizona's Petrified Forest, but it doesn't often happen. The Park Service also administers national historic sites like the homes of the presidents; national memorials such as New York's Federal Hall and Mount Rushmore in South Dakota; national military parks, including Gettysburg in Pennsylvania and Shiloh in Tennessee; and national historical parks from Independence Hall in Philadelphia to Appomattox Courthouse in Virginia. The Park Service is also responsible for ten national seashores and four national lakeshores. It operates four national parkways, a dozen national rivers, seventeen national recreation areas, and ten parks that are still waiting to be classified. It's enough to take your breath away. But that's the best thing about the national parks in the United States and in Canada. And thanks to them we can all breathe a little easier, and they come with a guarantee that our grandchildren will, too.

BELOW:
The Everglades is actually a river, carrying water from Lake Okeechobee to the upper end of Florida Bay, 100 miles (161 km) away. It varies in width from fifty to seventy miles (80 to 113 km), and is less than two feet (60 cm) in depth. It drops just seventeen feet (5 m) from one end to the other, which makes it one of the world's slowest-moving rivers. In fact, at some points, it seems to be standing still. In addition to the water from the lake, it is fed by some fifty-five inches (140 cm) of rain each year, most of it falling in late summer and early fall. Just before the rainy season, more than 90 percent of the land is exposed.

Maine (1929)
44 square miles
(114 square kilometers)

ACADIA

PREVIOUS PAGE:

The lighthouse at Bass Harbor Head marks the southernmost point of Mount Desert Island. It is a white tower attached to the lighthouse-keeper's home and has been in service since 1858. At the time it was put into operation, the island was already a retreat of the wealthy, who had become bored with the social scene down the coast at Newport, Rhode Island. From 1900 until the beginning of World War I, it was the vacation destination of choice for families with names like Rockefeller, Vanderbilt, and Morgan.

ABOVE:

Acadia's landscape is made even more beautiful in the fall when the maples turn brilliant red against the granite outcroppings. The 13- by 16- mile (21- by 26-km) island was orginally named Isle des Mounts Deserts, "Island of Bare Mountains," by Samuel de Champlain, who discovered it in 1604. The highest of them, Mount Cadillac, was named for the French nobleman who later moved from here to the shores of the Great Lakes and was further immortalized by an automobile company. At 1,530 feet (466 m), it is the highest point on the Eastern seaboard.

RIGHT:

Sand Beach, though sheltered in Newport Cove on the south side of the island, is almost too cold for swimming at any time of the year. Although putting your toe in the water at Acadia isn't among the park's pleasures, the sea is at its most dramatic on the rocky coast of Mount Desert Island. There are also 150 miles (241 km) of footpaths cutting through Acadia's valleys and climbing to the tops of its hills. It is also possible to take a week-long windjammer cruise or to camp in the forest, where you can be among the first to catch a sunrise over the United States.

South Dakota (1978)
985 square miles
(2,551 square kilometers)

BADLANDS

LEFT:
Thirty-seven million years ago, soft clay and sandstone were carried here by streams from the Black Hills to the west and by winds from the prairies. The sediment became a vast plain that was eventually carved by streams into gullies and canyons. The plain teemed with life, including such creatures as sabre-toothed tigers and the early ancestors of camels and horses, whose fossilized bones make the Badlands a kind of graveyard that is still giving up secrets of a prehistoric world.

∞

OVERLEAF LEFT:
Visitors who see the Badlands for the first time are usually surprised when the countryside suddenly changes from endless miles of rolling grass to a fantastic landscape of canyons, buttes, and gullies. The maze of pinnacles and escarpments changes just as abruptly on the other side of the depression to become grassland again. But in between is a valley of almost unearthly beauty where time seems to stand still.

∞

OVERLEAF RIGHT:
The colorful mounds still support animal life, though some species found it difficult to survive the advance of civilization. When settlers first arrived, the hills were home to herds of elk and bison, which then completely disappeared from the scene. The good news is that the bison have come back and so have the bighorn sheep; and thanks to the protection of the Park System, they aren't likely to go away again. Bobcats and badgers, prairie dogs and foxes, and other small mammals never went away.

The name Badlands was given to this area by early pioneers who found it difficult to cross. They hadn't seen anything yet, of course, since the Rocky Mountains are due west. Good roads make the trip quite easy these days and the roadside views include a forty-mile (64-km) collection of razorlike ridges, as well as a painted landscape of deep canyons and gulches in the remains of what was a lush swamp eons ago.

© Stan Osolinski/FPG International

RIGHT:

Banff is Canada's oldest national park. It was created out of a dispute among railway builders over the potential exploitation of mineral hot springs they had discovered during construction of the Canadian Pacific Railroad. The government settled the argument by declaring the springs the property of the people. The park grew by leaps and bounds after that and the railroad, which had picked the spot as a convenient way to cross the Rocky Mountains, discovered that it had also created an important destination along the way.

© Stan Osolinski/M.L. Dembinsky Jr. Photo Assoc.

Alberta (1885)
2,585 square miles
(6,695 square kilometers)

BANFF

ABOVE:

In Banff and the other Rocky Mountain parks, prairie grasslands and alpine forests often share the same hillsides and flowers, in much the same way that firewood thrives alongside pines and firs. Above the treeline, vegetation is stunted by the almost constant wind, but delicate alpine flowers grow among the glaciers on the high peaks. The succession of plant life on the mountainsides almost exactly duplicates the variety of specialization that takes place from south to north toward the Arctic Circle.

RIGHT:

All of Banff's lakes are tinged with a turquoise color due to minerals carried down the mountainsides by melting glaciers. The lakes come in an almost endless variety of sizes and shapes, each reflecting spectacular mountain peaks. No one has ever suggested a beauty contest among Banff's lakes, probably because any time you think you've found the most beautiful one, you're likely to find one even more beautiful a few miles away. But wouldn't it be rewarding to make judging such a contest your life's work?

Texas (1944)
1,080 square miles
(2,797 square kilometers)

BIG BEND

© Tom Algire/Tom Stack & Associates

© Matt Bradley/Tom Stack & Associates

LEFT:

Long before Big Bend was formally mapped, it was a refuge for train robbers, bandits, and other desperadoes, who knew that not even Judge Roy Bean, who was "the law west of the Pecos," would dare to penetrate their hiding place. As recently as 1916, the Mexican revolutionary Pancho Villa led a raid into the United States through Boquillas Canyon, the largest of three canyons the Rio Grande River has carved on its curving course.

∞

OPPOSITE PAGE:

The Rio Grande River makes a sweeping 100-mile (161-km) U-shaped turn about 400 miles (644 km) west of San Antonio, creating a landscape even Texans are hard-pressed to find superlatives for. It is dominated by the Chisos Mountains, which change color as the sun moves across them. Big Bend is possibly the wildest of all the national parks—the early Spanish explorers, who weren't intimidated by anything, passed around it rather than through it. Even the Texas Rangers found it impenetrable, and it wasn't until 1899 that Robert T. Hill, leading a geological survey, became the first prospector to map it.

LEFT:

The Rio Grande flows beneath sheer rock walls as much as 1,500-feet (457-m) high. In spite of the hostile environment, more than 1,300 different kinds of plants, many unique to this area, grow within the park. Cowboys who once punched cattle here claimed that every one of them "sticks, stings, or stinks," but the flora survived the bad press and peacefully coexists with such animals as pronghorn, peccaries, armadillos, and white-tailed deer, not to mention park visitors who find them all wonders to behold. Among the park's wildlife are no less than one hundred different kinds of grasshoppers, even though grass is in relatively short supply.

RIGHT:

In 1859, the United States Army used the Big Bend area as a proving ground for its projected camel corps, which it hoped would give them the edge in moving heavy supplies to outposts in the Southwest. The project was abandoned when the Civil War distracted the military planners. The desert sands as well as the rocky mesas at Big Bend were created from the sediment of a prehistoric inland sea, which later became swamps and tropical forests that sheltered dinosaurs and crocodiles five times bigger than their descendants. Remains of the flying reptile known as pterodactyl, which flew off into extinction more than 60 million years ago, have also been found in Big Bend's rocks.

RIGHT:

Prickly pear and other spiny desert plants make walking a less-than-pleasant experience for visitors who neglect to remember their hiking boots. Nevertheless, few experiences compare with a hike through the desert country, and Big Bend has more than 350 miles (563 km) of trails to experience. For visitors who prefer to see it on horseback, the trip along the south rim of the Boquillas Canyon, which takes a full day, takes in the complete Big Bend experience through thick forests to the top, where the view from 7,200 feet (2,195 m) includes the river, the desert, and distant mountains.

© J. Messerschmidt/FPG International

Utah (1924)
56 square miles
(145 square kilometers)

BRYCE CANYON

LEFT:
The hoodoos that rise up from the canyon's floor have almost all been created by the action of water. At night the temperature routinely drops below freezing and moisture trapped in the rocks is turned to ice that melts in the hot sun during the day. The alternate freezing and thawing causes the rocks to move and pile up. Modern visitors imagine city skylines when they see them, but the Paiute Indians had a more romantic notion. They decided that the birds and animals living in the canyon had the magical power to make themselves look human, but that a powerful god who was displeased with them turned them into stone.

LEFT:

The shale and sandstone that has eroded into fantastic shapes in Bryce Canyon is sediment from a huge inland lake that covered much of the Southwest some 70 million years ago. Mountain streams that fed the lake brought calcium, which strengthened the rocks, as well as iron deposits, which gave them a reddish color, and manganese, adding touches of blue. There are dozens of views along the twenty-mile (32-km) dead end road that enters the park from the north. It doesn't take long to get to the end, but those views can be distracting. One of the earliest visitors to Bryce reported that he was so enraptured by the view that the sun went down before he could be dragged from it.

ABOVE:

In 1872, an explorer noted that Bryce Canyon's "standing obelisks, prostrate columns, shattered capitals all bring vividly before the mind suggestions of the work of giant hands, a race of genii now chained up in a spell of enchantment while their structures are falling in ruins." Ebenezer Bryce, who tried to establish a farm here a few years later, couldn't think of anything better to say about it than the eighteen-mile (29-km) long canyon is "a hell of a place to lose a cow." Early in this century a promoter offered ten dollars to any visitor who could honestly say the canyon wasn't awe-inspiring. Windowed rocks like these guaranteed he didn't often have to make good on his promise.

CAPE BRETON HIGHLANDS

RIGHT:

Cape Breton's rivers and streams are a paradise for fishermen who enjoy the challenge of landing salmon or trout. Just as challenging is the eighteen-hole Ingonish Golf Course, one of the world's greatest. For those looking for a way to escape life's challenges, there are beaches to lie on and hiking trails to wander along, both on the the coast and through the interior. There are also 850 campsites, ranging from landscaped sites with available hot showers to places where roughing it takes on a whole new meaning.

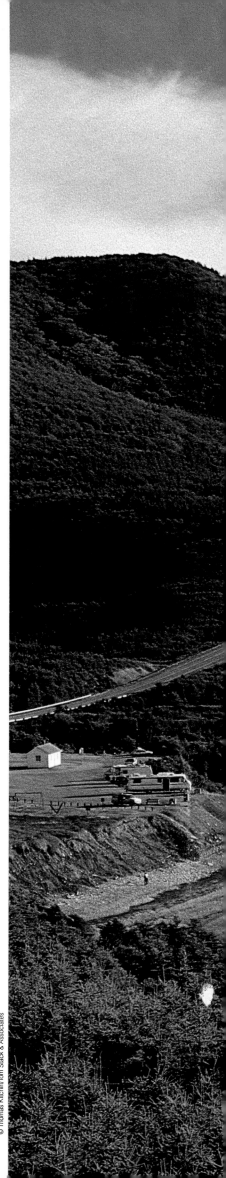

RIGHT:

The Cabot Trail circles the island on a 184-mile (296-km) roller coaster-like route that winds along cliffs overlooking the sea, through deep forests on the sides of steep mountains, and across the flower-strewn moors. About half the journey is through the park itself, leaving the wilderness at a point where quaint fishing villages line sandy beaches. Along the way, in addition to the spectacular scenery, a driver is likely to be distracted by the sight of a moose, a black bear, a red fox, or representatives of the 230 species of birds that make their home in the Highlands.

© Ann & Myron Sutton/FPG International

New Mexico (1930)
184 square miles
(478 square kilometers)

CARLSBAD CAVERNS

LEFT:
*All of Carlsbad's rooms are
dramatically lighted, but the
most memorable part of the
guided tour comes when the
guide turns off all the lights.
There is no experience that
quite compares to the total
darkness and eerie silence the
simple flicking of a switch
creates. Even with the lights
turned on, you experience a
total loss of any sense of
direction. All you know for sure
is that the surface is straight
up. Or is it?*

ABOVE:

The ceiling of the fourteen-acre (6-ha) Big Room with its giant stalagmite, Twin Domes, is 285 feet (87 m) high. It is one of Carlsbad's most impressive features and can be reached directly from the surface by elevator. However, it is much more impressive as a highlight of the four-hour, three-mile walking tour that includes visits to rooms with such fanciful names as Fairyland, Papoose Room, Mirror Lake, and the Rock of Ages.

RIGHT:

In spite of the fact that more than fifty feet (15 m) of snow falls on Crater Lake each winter, the park is open all year, providing snowshoers and cross-country skiers with a beautiful backdrop. Even a driving rainstorm can't diminish it. But the best time of all is at sunrise, when the water is smooth and unruffled, reflecting the cliffs that rise nearly 2,000 feet (610 m) around it.

Oregon (1902)
648 square miles
(1,678 square kilometers)

CRATER LAKE

RIGHT:
Crater Lake fills twenty-six square miles (67 sq km) of the caldera created by the eruption of Mount Mazuma more than 6,000 years ago. At 1,932 feet (589 m), it is the deepest lake in North America. There is no outlet or inlet, and its intensely blue water is replenished by rain and melting snow, which equals the amount lost through seepage and evaporation. Wizard Island, a cone of cinders rising 760 feet (232 m) above the lake, is the tip of a 6,940-foot (2,115-m) mountain. It is a favorite destination of boat trips and the best place to see nearby Phantom Ship Island and the volcanic formations in the caldera's walls.

© Ellis-Sawyer/FPG International

ABOVE:

Among the park's wonders are the Pinnacles, including the Pumice Desert, which was created by a rush of lava from the exploding volcano. The needlelike spires are also made of volcanic pumice, rising from the floor of the canyon of Wheeler Creek. The mountain peaks in the park include the 8,926-foot (2,721-m) Mount Scott, and on a clear day the 14,162-foot (4,317-m) Mount Shasta, 105 miles (169 km) away in California, becomes part of the scenery.

RIGHT:

The glacier-covered Alaska Range is a perfect backdrop for the wildflowers that fill the valleys in late summer and early fall. The show is a short one, though. The valleys are usually covered with snow by mid-September and stay that way until almost the end of May. Denali is open all year, but during the long winter the easiest way to get around is by dogsled. Even on the coldest days, and it does get cold at Denali, caribou paw at the snow to feast on lichens, and small birds peck at the frozen trees to find tasty dormant insects. Park rangers take advantage of the snow cover to get into areas where the tundra is too fragile for summertime work.

© Sharon Cummings/M.L. Dembinsky Jr. Photo Assoc.

Alaska (1917, as Mount
McKinley National Park)
3,030 square miles
(7,847 square kilometers)

DENALI

RIGHT:

The reindeer that Santa Claus made famous are smaller cousins of the caribou, one of the more frequently seen denizens of Denali. Their antlers protect them from most predators, but wolves often ignore the danger. Sometimes one or two of them will attack from the front, distracting the caribou while the rest of the pack moves in from behind. The favored method is for a pack of fifteen or more to surround the larger animal and drive it into a snowbank or thicket where it can't escape their sharp teeth and strong jaws.

RIGHT:

The gold at the end of the rainbow in Denali is the color of caribou, creatures that seem to be everywhere you look. Denali is one of North America's largest wildlife preserves, designated as a United Nations Biosphere Reserve, where scientists have a rare opportunity to study subarctic plants and animals. It is one of the few places in the world where wolves are fully protected, and where visitors are well-advised to take precautions to protect themselves from the large population of grizzly bears. As an added form of wildlife protection, private vehicles are prohibited from most parts of the park, and free bus transportation is provided.

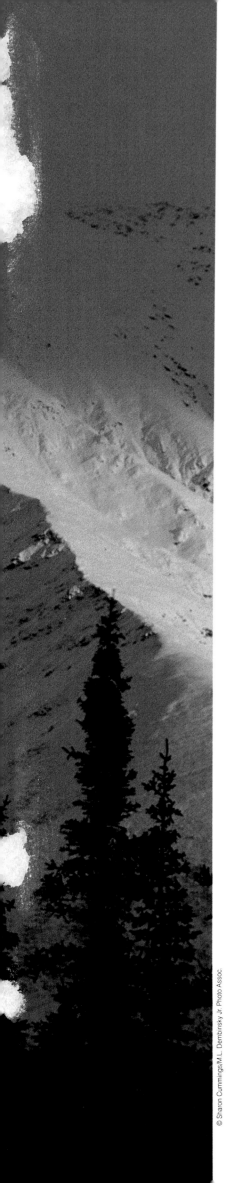

LEFT:
Dall's sheep, which are found throughout the Rocky Mountains, are noted for the ram's magnificent curved horns which form a "C" shape, called a curl, when viewed from the side—which is generally the safest way to view one. The ewes have shorter, more slender horns that curve only slightly.

LEFT:
In midsummer, the sun shines twenty-four hours a day at Denali. At times of the year when the sun rises and sets, the mountains are bathed in a reddish alpenglow during the pre-dawn and twilight hours.

The weather at Mount McKinley is capricious and it is quite possible for a visitor at Denali to stay in the park for weeks and never actually see the mist-shrouded, 20,320 foot (6,194 m) mountain, the highest in North America. The word "denali," which became the park's name in 1980, means "great one" in the language of the Athapaskan Indians who were the first to see it.

Florida (1947)
423 square miles
(1,096 square kilometers)

EVERGLADES

RIGHT:

They sing songs about the moon over Miami, but sunrise over the Everglades is a much more romantic experience. The Everglades is essentially a sea of sawgrass, but tree islands called hammocks rise from spots where the underwater limestone shelf rises enough to create dry land or dips deep enough to trap sediment and peat that give roots a toehold. In some places, willows thrive around deep holes and their leaves provide a kind of landfill that eventually supports larger trees.

ABOVE:

The American alligator is the beast most visitors to the Everglades have in mind when they plan their trip. They are cold-blooded, absorbing warmth from the sun, and have the energy-saving habit of lying motionless most of the time. They don't eat more than twice a week and have been known to go as long as six months between meals. But don't let all that fool you, they can move like lightning when they have to, and don't mind attacking creatures larger than themselves.

∞

RIGHT:

There are 326 species of birds living in the Everglades, including more bald eagles than in the Rocky Mountain parks. The anhinga, which resembles a cormorant, is often seen perched in trees with outspread wings to get a jump on a passing fish, which it spears with its pointed bill.

Quebec (1970)
93 square miles
(241 square kilometers)

FORILLON

PREVIOUS PAGE:
The sandstone formations of the Gaspésian Mountains make up the northernmost end of the Appalachian chain, which ranges south from this point all the way to Alabama. Geologically, the peninsula is one of the oldest spots of land on the earth. The rugged coastline and virtually untouched inland forests make it seem like a land that time forgot in spite of the fact that Portuguese fishermen found their way here as early as the thirteenth century, and the Vikings explored it even before that. The peninsula is completely unspoiled and seems to be waiting to be discovered all over again.

∞

LEFT:
The limestone cliffs of Cap Bon Ami are spectacular from any angle, but they are at their most dramatic from the beach below, which can be reached by a foot path. Forillon is at the tip of Gaspé Peninsula, which juts out into the Gulf of St. Lawrence. The cliffs attract thousands of sea birds that nest here during the summer months. Before Jacques Cartier claimed the land for France in 1534, it was a favorite summer campground for Iroquois and Micmac Indians, who were attracted by the abundance of fish and marine mammals. It is still a favorite spot for seals, and whale watchers are seldom disappointed when they look out to sea from the high cliffs.

Alaska (1980)
12,500 square miles
(32,374 square kilometers)

GATES OF THE ARCTIC

RIGHT:
When Bob Marshall began rambling through this countryside in the 1930s, he said "there is something glorious in traveling beyond the ends of the earth." The glory hasn't diminished. The mountain peaks average about 6,000 feet (1,829 m), but because they are treeless, it's difficult to estimate individual heights. Marshall was especially impressed by a 5,550-foot (1,692-m) peak he named Frigid Crags and its next-door neighbor, Boreal Mountain, 6,666 feet (2,032 m) high. He said that together, with the Koyukuk River flowing north between them, they were the Gates of the Arctic.

LEFT:

There are beaten paths in this park, but not many of them. Gates of the Arctic is a true wilderness, with almost no traces of any human influence. Many of its delightful waterfalls, valleys, and mountain peaks have never been given a name and don't appear on maps. The surprises are often pleasant, but sometimes even well-experienced outdoorsmen find their path barred by unexpected obstacles. Most find it an advantage, and say it adds to their understanding of the meaning of total wilderness, as well as being a means of protecting the fragile environment by keeping it mysterious and slightly menacing. Gates of the Arctic is clearly not a playground for casual day-trippers.

LEFT:

Gates of the Arctic, four times the size of Yellowstone, adjoins the 10,300-square-mile (26,676-sq-km) Noatak National Preserve to the west and the 29,680-square-mile (76,868-sq-km) Arctic National Wildlife Refuge to the east. Together they cover the entire Brooks Range above the Arctic Circle. It was largely unexplored before 1929, when Bob Marshall, a founder of the Wilderness Society, climbed its mountains and explored its icefields, and coined the name "Gates of the Arctic." He began a one-man campaign to create a national park here, and he set his sights on the entire territory north of the Yukon River. What we got is much less, but the protected area is bigger than the states of Pennsylvania and New Jersey combined. Wildlife is protected here, but not from nature itself.

Montana (1910)
1,583 square miles
(4,100 square kilometers)

GLACIER

LEFT:

The fifty-mile-long (80-km) Going to The Sun Road allows visitors to study glacier-carved peaks and endless meadows of wildflowers. However, most of the park can only be seen on foot. Glacier has one of the most extensive networks of trails of any national park, more than 700 miles (1,127 km) of them, many offering a textbook definition of the word "solitude." Among the fifty-seven species of animals that live there are black bears and even grizzlies in the higher elevations; it isn't uncommon for hikers to attach bells to their feet to reduce the possibility of surprising one.

ABOVE:

Mount Reynolds is one of the peaks that the Lewis and Clark expedition spotted on its way to Oregon in 1804. Like the rest of the territory preserved at Glacier, it is exactly the same today as it was then. This is one of the most rugged, unspoiled spots anywhere in the United States' Rocky Mountains and, in the opinion of some, the most beautiful. The park contains more than fifty glaciers and 200 lakes, some of which give the impression no human being has dipped a toe into the water.

RIGHT:
The four-mile- (6-km-) long ridge of rock called the Garden Wall marks the Continental Divide, which runs through Glacier Park. East of the Divide, the woodlands are filled with lodgepole pines, Englemann spruce, and Douglas firs. To the west, where there is more moisture, the forests are thicker and the trees noticeably taller. The trees that grow there include hemlock and red cedar, ponderosa pines, and alpine firs along with cottonwood, larch, and white birch.

© Christopher Bain

**Arizona (1919)
2,165 square miles
(5,607 square kilometers)**

GRAND CANYON

LEFT:
A sign at the edge of the south rim warns hikers they've reached the trail's end. Though some of the letters are missing, most people get the message that the next step is likely to be a long one. One of the Grand Canyon's vertical walls is a sheer 3,000-foot (914-m) drop, more than the combined height of Chicago's Sears Tower and New York's World Trade Center. However, the drop from most spots along the south rim is comparatively gentle and there are guard rails at all observation points.

∞

OVERLEAF LEFT:
The view from the edge of Mather Point is like a vision of the ends of the earth. Though you can see for miles, even on the clearest day the view encompasses only about a quarter of the 1.2 million-acre (486,000-ha) park. When the clouds part, the view also includes glimpses of the Colorado River, 4,600 feet (1,402 m) down. The river began cutting the Grand Canyon some 600 million years ago and continues today. It has about 2,000 feet (610 m) to go before the bottom reaches sea level and the force of gravity finally tames the river.

ABOVE:

The first official government survey of the Grand Canyon in 1857 concluded that "ours has been the first and doubtless will be the last party of whites to visit this profitless locality. It seems intended by nature that the Colorado River along the greater portion of its majestic way shall be forever unvisited and undisturbed." Some three million people a year prove the survey wrong by visiting.

∞

LEFT:

Fog is not among the natural wonders to be expected this close to the Arizona desert, but when it rolls over the rim of the Grand Canyon it adds a spectacular dimension to a place that never seems in need of added drama. Fog rolls in during the winter months when the north rim is usually snowbound; snow sometimes falls on the warmer south rim, too. The temperature at the bottom of the Canyon, which stays in the high 90s (35° C) all summer long, rarely drops below 70° (21° C) even when snow is falling up above.

© M.L. Dembinsky, Jr.

North Carolina, Tennessee
(1926)
800 square miles
(2,072 square kilometers)

**GREAT SMOKY
MOUNTAINS**

LEFT:
The moist climate of the Smokies fills the forests with hardy dogwood as well as brilliantly colored rhododendrons, laurel, and azaleas, which bloom through mid-July. There are some 1,300 varieties of trees and shrubs in the park, more than exist in all of Europe, and almost any of which could rate at least honorable mention in nature's beauty contest. The rainfall, which reaches up to 100 inches (254 cm) in some spots, encourages hardwood trees to grow to an almost unnatural size; rhododendrons often reach twenty-five feet (8 m) into the air. At the edges of the forest are hundreds of sun-drenched meadows filled with the butterflies attracted by thousands of wildflowers.

ABOVE:

Before the park was established, most of the territory was owned by timber companies, but as many as 6,000 small farms settled there, too. Their abandoned homesteads have beome part of the charm of the Smoky Mountains, where there are surprises at nearly every turn. Like most national parks, the best rewards are to be found on foot, but for those who prefer to commune with nature from behind the wheel of a car, taped tours are available, including one in Cherokee, the first language spoken here. The descendants of the Native Americans live on the Qualla Reservation adjoining the park, the largest reservation east of the Mississippi.

RIGHT:

There are sixteen mountain peaks more than 6,000 feet (1,828 m) high within the Great Smoky Mountain national park. It is the highest section of the Appalachian Mountains, often called the roof of eastern America. The mountains rise above the almost constant mist that both gives them their name and maintains the moisture that makes the forests so lush. The Smokies were created by upheavals in the earth millions of years ago, and they escaped the erosion that affected the northern section of the chain during the age of the great glaciers.

HAWAII VOLCANOES

RIGHT:

The volcanoes themselves are the park's main attractions, but its coastal section is rewarding, too. The coast is still forming as hot lava pours into the sea, and even as steam rises from the rocks, the heavy waves are at work molding them into fantastic shapes. The lava flows from Mauna Loa alone have added more than 2,000 square miles (5,180 sq km) to the Big Island of Hawaii. The park extends over to the island of Maui where the dormant volcano, Haleakala, is Hawaii's most-visited attraction. Within its twenty-one-mile (34-km) crater are cinder cones, caverns, and meadows filled with exotic flowers.

© Stan Osolinski/M.L. Dembinsky Jr. Photo Assoc.

RIGHT:

The fingers of black lava, which still seem fluid even after they've cooled, would appear at first glance to be completely hostile to any kind of plant life. Actually the lava is mineral-rich and will eventually support incredibly lush rain forests. Life begins almost immediately when shoots of ohia lehua begin to appear in the still-warm rifts. Before long, the bleak landscape will be filled with giant tree ferns and tall ohia as well as flowering plants. The cycle may soon begin all over again as the volcano continues its work.

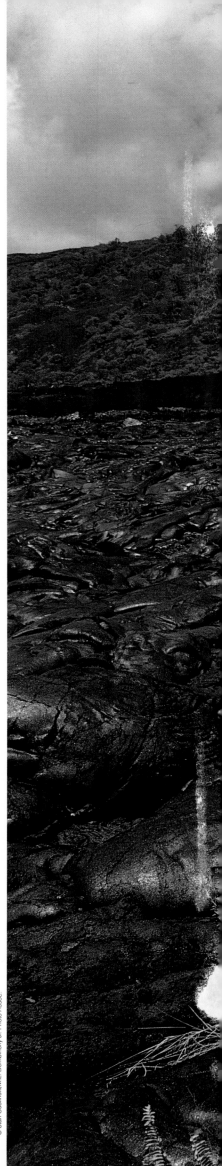

© Stan Osolinski/M.L. Dembinsky Jr. Photo Assoc.

LEFT:
"I have seen Vesuvius," wrote Mark Twain, "but it was a mere toy, a soup kettle compared to this." He also said that watching an eruption of Kilauea amounted to a revelation: It was the first time he was able to visualize the pillar of fire that guided the ancient Israelites across the desert. Kilauea erupted fifty times during the 1980s. In 1985, a new cone 700 feet (213 m) high was created. The 4,090-foot (1,247-m) volcano is actually a vent in the side of the 13,680-foot (4,170-m) Mauna Loa, but they erupt independently of each other. Kilauea's crater covers more than four square miles (10 sq km), slightly larger than that of Mauna Loa.

HOT SPRINGS

RIGHT:

About a million gallons (3,785,000 l) of thermal water with an average temperature of 143 degrees F (62° C), flow from forty-seven springs within the park each day. Some of it is channeled through this fountain in the Visitor Center courtyard, but most is piped to bathhouses, where it is cooled for visitors to "take the waters." People have been seeking the soothing effects of the water of the hot springs since the Native Americans called truces in their wars to relax in ceremonial steam baths. It became a Federal Reservation in 1832, forty years before Yellowstone became the first national park.

Alberta (1907)
4,200 square miles
(10,878 square kilometers)

JASPER

PREVIOUS PAGE, RIGHT:
The Athabaska Glacier at the southern end of Jasper Park is a tongue of the Columbia Icefield, the largest sheet of prehistoric ice on the North American continent below the Arctic Circle. The park was named for a trapper who operated on the fringes of the glacier in the 1800s. The Hudson's Bay Company traded in moose and caribou hides in the area, and in the 1850s nearby Yellowhead Pass became a major route to the gold fields across the mountains.

ABOVE:
Jasper is almost completely comprised of high mountains, but the less than 13 percent of its territory that is flatland is unusually lush thanks to the rivers and creeks that are constantly fed by melting glaciers. There are more than 600 miles (966 km) of hiking trails within the park, perfect for cross-country skiing and snowshoeing in winter. There are also ten campgrounds with more than 1,800 spaces available.

RIGHT:
Maligne Lake is the largest glacial lake in the Canadian Rockies, a mile (1.6 km) above sea level and surrounded by ice-covered mountains rising up another 10,000 feet (3,048 m). It is seventeen miles (27 km) long with a fifty-mile (80-km) shoreline. Though it is one of the scenic wonders of the continent, its name translates from the French as "bad." It was given to the Maligne River, which formed the lake, by a French missionary who found the ford at the junction of the Maligne and Athabaska Rivers nothing less than hellish. The full impact of Maligne Lake is best experienced by boat. Its shoreline is punctuated by otherwise inaccessible bays, waterfalls, and icefalls.

74

Alaska (1980)
10,915 square miles
(28,269 square kilometers)

KATMAI

RIGHT:

Salmon fishing is one of the reasons people brave Katmai's strong winds and drenching rainstorms known as williwaws, and fight mosquitoes that seem as big as sparrows. Sometimes, though, a fisherman has to wait until the real pros have their pick of the catch. A fully-grown brown bear is more than eight feet (240 cm) tall and every inch is muscle. Usually, the only creatures that challenge them in their salmon feasts are the bald eagles that nest in the park.

© Lee Kuhn/FPG International

RIGHT:

Brown bear cubs would do almost anything for a fish dinner. But though their instincts tell them that fish are the tastiest of all dishes, they don't know instinctively how to catch them. It's their mother's job to teach them, and if mom's not around they have to stand and wait as they watch all those succulent creatures swim past.

© John Shaw/Tom Stack & Associates

Colorado (1906)
80 square miles
(207 square kilometers)

MESA VERDE

PREVIOUS PAGE:
Benjamin Wetherill, a silver prospector, staked his claim on Mesa Verde in 1879. When it didn't produce any riches, he turned to cattle ranching. His sons stumbled on the cliff dwellings a few years later while tracking down some stray calves and soon after they went into the tourist business. They knew they had discovered a treasure that went far beyond arrowheads and baskets, and in 1895 stopped selling souvenirs in favor of encouraging legitimate archaelogical expeditions. The result was that the clues to the everyday life of the Anasazi were preserved intact. Research is still continuing, but no archaeologist has yet come up with the reason these elaborate homes were abandoned so suddenly.

∞

RIGHT:
With their city protected by the overhanging cliffs, the Anasazi were completely safe from marauding enemies. They seem to have felt so safe, in fact, that their pueblos were built without doors. They constructed dams and a sophisticated irrigation system which made their farms productive, and they even had domesticated animals for food. But their idyllic life came to an abrupt end about the year 1300. The Anasazi simply vanished without a trace; no one knows where they went or why they left. They seem to have intended to come back. Seed corn and clothing, weapons and pottery, and intricate jewelry was left behind. It was all still there, untouched, when a party of explorers found the mesa in 1874.

Washington (1899)
378 square miles
(979 square kilometers)

MOUNT RAINIER

LEFT:

"Regal" is the word most often used to describe Mount Rainier. Reflected in a mountain lake, the only word that suits it is "sublime." The mountain is part of the so-called volcanic ring of fire that circles the Pacific, and not too many years ago made its presence felt in the eruptions of nearby Mount St. Helens. But Rainier's fire seems to have gone out, and the mountain is covered with ice the year round.

∞

OVERLEAF LEFT:

There are sixty-two lakes within the park, including Reflection Lake, a short drive from the Paradise Visitor Center at the base of Mount Rainier. It is unforgettable at sunrise, but another visitor center on the other side of the mountain is an even better place to watch the sun come up. It is the highest point in the entire state of Washington, reached by a paved road, appropriately called Sunrise. This is also the best possible place for a close-up look at Emmons Glacier, the largest in the United States outside Alaska.

ABOVE:
Mount Rainier itself is a 14,408-foot (4,392-m) volcano. It may look peaceful in the moonlight, but steam still rises from its vents. Though it has been dormant since 1870, geologists say that one eruption centuries ago blew 2,000 feet (610 m) from its top, an event, they hasten to add, that isn't likely to be soon repeated.

∞

LEFT:
The Paradise River is flanked by a trail perfect for a short hike, with charming waterfalls among its rewards. Not far away, a loop trail, known as the Trail of Shadows, meanders among beaver ponds and through the old settlement of Longmire. There are more than 300 miles (483 km) of trails within the park including the ninety-mile (145-km) Wonderland Trail that circles the base of Mount Rainier, through forests and subalpine meadows and along creeks and rivers. If a ninety-mile (145-km) hike seems too short, there are other trails crisscrossing it.

Washington (1968)
789 square miles
(2,043 square kilometers)

NORTH CASCADES

RIGHT:

In the middle of the last century, loggers began stripping the valleys of the Cascades, and in the 1920s hydroelectric projects began changing the face of the land. In the 1950s, the Sierra Club and others mounted a campaign to preserve some of what was left as a national park. The compromise that followed created a two-unit park, separated by a national recreation area. The northern section, filled with glaciers, high mountains, and hidden valleys, extends to the Canadian border. The lower part includes a dramatic glacier-carved canyon.

LEFT:

The North Cascades Highway leading into the park is usually closed during the winter because of heavy snow. However, visitors who take the passenger ferry down Lake Chelan or fly in on a float plane take back memories of scenery like this from their cross-country ski tours. The lake is up to two miles (3 km) wide, and is set in a trough surrounded by deep forests and high mountains. The ferry trip is an adventure at any time of the year.

ABOVE:

The hundreds of jagged, glacier-covered peaks in the North Cascades make the park a mecca for mountain climbers — even the most experienced find plenty of challenges. Most areas of the park are accessible only on foot, which many say is what gives the North Cascades its special charm. Human visitors can share the deep, forested valleys and the high mountains with their wild residents. One of the most popular hiking trails cuts through Easy Pass, whose name may be misleading if you're a tenderfoot.

ABOVE:

*Misty mornings are an
important part of Olympic's
charm, and it's a rare day when
the mountains aren't shrouded
in fog at sunrise. The park
includes North America's only
temperate zone rain forest, with
an average precipitation of 140
inches (356 cm) a year. But
that's only on the western slope
of the mountains, where the
November-to-March rainy
season encourages Douglas firs
and western red cedars to grow.
On the northeast side,
conditions are the driest on the
West Coast, except for the
deserts of California.*

∞

RIGHT:

*There are fifty-three species of
mammals in Olympic's
wilderness, including mule
deer. The park also has the
country's largest herd of
Roosevelt elk, a population
estimated at 5,000. It is home to
black bears and hard-working
beavers, mountain lions and
snowshoe rabbits.*

Washington (1938)
1,431 square miles
(3,706 square kilometers)

OLYMPIC

The jagged, snowy peaks surrounding 7,956-foot (2,425-m) Mount Olympus usually make it hard to see. Together, they form a landscape of barren, snow-covered rock, rivers, lakes, and alpine meadows. It is the most rugged mountain scenery in the American West, and is visible from far out at sea. The mountains were given their name, in fact, by the navigator of an English ship that was sailing past in 1788.

ABOVE:

The Olympic Mountains were discovered in 1774 by Spanish explorers, who apparently weren't too impressed. More than a century passed before others came for a closer look. What they found were evergreen-filled valleys ringed by a snow-covered ridge of mountains averaging more than 5,000 feet (1,524 m) above sea level. The height becomes more meaningful when you consider that part of Olympic National Park is at sea level. It includes fifty-seven miles (92 km) of unspoiled Pacific Ocean coastline where seals sun on the rocks.

RIGHT:

Arizona was organized as a territory, but was more than fifteen years away from becoming a state when President Theodore Roosevelt signed the legislation designating the Petrified Forest, then called Chalcedony, a national monument. Then more than sixty-five years passed before it became a national park. In terms of the forces that created this natural wonder and continue to change it, those years represent less than the wink of an eye.

RIGHT:

Red is the predominant color of the Painted Desert, one of the most beautiful areas in Petrified Forest National Park. It was created millions of years ago when a change in climate caused a mantle of limestone to erode, uncovering petrified wood and fossils that had been buried under it. When the formation dried out, iron deposits in the mud oxidized, creating a variety of hues that range from dull to brilliant. Alkalai patches add additional colors and the sun intensifies them. The desert is at its best in late afternoon when the shadows from the rock formations deepen the colors.

RIGHT:

The bands in the rocks are caused by different layers of sediment and seem to come in every color of the rainbow. The park's chief attraction is the fossilized wood that is strewn everywhere. Scientists say that the normal rate of decay of the tree trunks was slowed here because they were under water, with no oxygen to promote rotting. The water was also rich in silica, which soaked into the wood creating quartz crystals that were colored by traces of minerals.

California (1968)
89 square miles
(231 square kilometers)

REDWOOD

© Thomas Kitchin/Tom Stack & Associates

PREVIOUS PAGE:
The redwood is the tallest tree in the world, averaging more than 200 feet (61 m) with trunks twenty feet (6 m) in diameter. The tallest of them is 367.8 feet (112 m) high and its nearest competitor is only six inches (15 cm) shorter. Both are in Redwood National Park, along Redwood Creek, where they have been standing for more than 400 years. The big trees once grew in Canada, Western Europe, and England as well as northern California, where the thick summer fogs from the ocean and a moderate year-round temperature provide a perfect environment for them.

∞

RIGHT:
Redwood ranges from an elevation of 1,500 feet (457 m) down to the level of the sea. The rocky coast that forms the thirty-mile (48-km) boundary of the park attracts seals and surf fishermen, but swimmers find their pleasure on Mill Creek or the Smith River. The national park includes three California state parks: Jedediah Smith, Del Norte Coast, and Prairie Creek, which will eventually be administered by the Department of the Interior. U.S. Route 101, a four-lane highway, runs for more than 380 miles (611 km) along the coast through stands of both sequoia and redwood trees.

Colorado (1915)
405 square miles
(1,049 square kilometers)

ROCKY MOUNTAIN

PREVIOUS PAGE:

With more than 100 mountain peaks over 10,000 feet (3,048 m) high, most of Rocky Mountain National Park is above the timberline. Trail Ridge Road, which crosses this easternmost point on the Continental Divide, is the highest paved highway in the United States. It is more than 11,000 feet (3,353 m) high for fifteen miles (24 km), with its high point the five-acre (2-ha) flat top of the 14,255-foot (4,345-m) Long's Peak. A short two-hour drive from Denver, the park attracts more than three million visitors a year, and as many as 700 cars an hour. The view covers as much as sixty square miles (155 sq km) from most points, and there are frequent turnoffs to enhance the pleasure. Incredible to most of us, the winding fifty-mile (80-km) road is a favorite challenge for bicyclists, who often move along faster than the cars, even on the uphill stretches.

ABOVE:

When the first explorers approached the front range of the Rockies, they weren't sure they were seeing mountains in the distance, and some members of the party insisted they were actually looking at huge banks of clouds. The mountains eventually gave them opportunities to get close enough to the clouds to reach out and touch them. Snow can be found in the park at most times of the year, and there are a half-dozen small glaciers. The climate varies according to where you are. The crest of the range is 9,000 feet (2,743 m) straight up from the plain.

RIGHT:

About a third of the park is covered with alpine tundra, more than any other below Alaska. Trees won't grow at these altitudes because there isn't enough moisture, but tiny plants have adapted to the hostile environment. The growing season lasts only about a month before they go dormant again and pull in half-developed flower buds, which will pick up where they left off the following year. Lichens and mosses grow in the crevices of rocks, and their debris is picked up by the wind and deposited in flat places, creating a thin layer of soil that allows other plants to take root. It takes hundreds of years to create a meadow like this one. On the other hand, it took more than 300 million years to build these spectacular mountains.

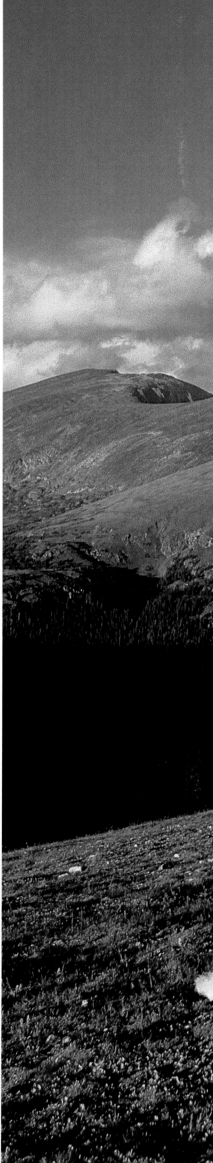

TUNNEL LOG

FELL DECEMBER 4, 1937
BASE DIAMETER 21 FEET
LENGTH 275 FEET
TUNNEL 8 FT. HIGH, 17 FT. WIDE

**California (1890)
604 square miles
(1,564 square kilometers)**

SEQUOIA

LEFT:

This tree fell across the road back in 1937. Its trunk is twenty-one feet (6.4 m) in diameter, and it was 275 feet (84 m) high. If it had been cut up into lumber, it would have provided enough boards to build thirty or forty houses. Fortunately, it was left where it fell, both as a memorial to itself and to dramatize the girth of an average-sized sequoia, which is sometimes hard to visualize even when you're standing at the base of one of these giants.

∞

OVERLEAF ABOVE:

The trail that leads to the crest of Morro Rock offers rewarding views of the ridges of the High Sierra. Morro Rock itself is one of the most impressive of all the range's monoliths. John Muir, whose writings galvanized the creation of Sequoia and Kings Canyon as well as Yosemite National Park, said that places like this were "fountains of life." Of the mountains themselves, he said they "should be called not the Nevada, or Snowy Range, but the Range of Light . . . the most divinely beautiful of all the mountain chains I have ever seen."

OPPOSITE PAGE:

For visitors looking toward the top of one of these trees, it's usually a sobering experience to think that some of them were growing here when the Roman Empire was established. Though humans have created higher structures, a building as tall as the average sequoia would have more than thirty-five floors. They are twice as high as the Statue of Liberty, and about the same height as the Capitol dome in Washington.

RIGHT:

Congress Trail meanders through groves of giant sequoia trees in what John Muir called "pure temple groves." The first settler to see them was a cattleman looking for good pastureland back in 1858. Over the next half-century, an entire forest of the big trees was completely destroyed by loggers, who often had to use dynamite to knock them down. Many of the trees were more than two thousand years old and had survived earthquakes, forest fires, and storms. Their destruction led to the creation of America's second national park, which put 250 square miles (647 sq km) of forest off-limits to the woodcutters in 1890. It was expanded to 604 square miles (1,564 sq km) thirty-six years later, and incorporated with Kings Canyon in 1940. The Mineral King Valley was added to the preserve in 1978.

Virginia (1926)
302 square miles
(782 square kilometers)

SHENANDOAH

RIGHT:

The park is one of the East's greatest wildlife preserves with a large population of deer, bear, fox, and other small mammals, as well as 200 different varieties of birds. During the spring and fall migration periods, the woods are filled with songbirds, but there are other seasonal rewards as well. In spring, the woods are filled with wildflowers, budding dogwood, azalea, and mountain laurel. The fall colors begin marching down from the mountaintops in mid-October and the hollows are filled with the flowers of asters and witch hazel.

∞

OPPOSITE PAGE:

An oasis in the Blue Ridge Mountains with forest-covered hills overlooking peaceful valleys, Shenandoah is only seventy-five miles (121 km) from Washington, D.C., and a hop, skip, and a jump from the most populated corner of the United States. The park is eighty miles (129 km) long and from two to thirteen miles (3 to 26 km) wide. The Skyline Drive covers its full length with seventy-five overlooks featuring inspiring views of the Shenandoah River Valley and the Allegheny Mountains beyond. Yet the best rewards are to be found on more than 500 miles (805 km) of foot trails. The Appalachian Trail winds ninety-six miles (154 km) through the park.

RIGHT:

About 95 percent of Shenandoah Park is covered with forests of oak, maple, hemlock, and some 100 other kinds of trees. They frame sparkling waterfalls and shelter streams that abound in trout. In most parts of the park, the landscape is exactly the same as it was before the settlers came, when the Native Americans named these hills Shenandoah, meaning "daughter of the stars."

© Pat & Bob Momich

© Pat Toops

Alberta (1898)
220 square miles
(570 square kilometers)

WATERTON LAKES

LEFT:
A glacier-fed stream flows through the multi-colored bed of seventy-foot- (21-m-) deep Red Rock Canyon at the heart of the Blakiston Valley. The canyon is one of the places in the park accessible by a paved road, but most of Waterton Lakes is best explored on foot over its hundred miles of graded trails. A seven-mile (11-km) trail from the Red Rock warden station leads through South Kootenay Pass into British Columbia. The red color of the rock on the canyon's walls is caused by iron-rich sediment from an ancient sea that covered the area millions of years ago.

ABOVE:
Waterton Lakes was incorporated into Glacier Park to form the world's first International Peace Park in 1932, due to urging by the Rotary Clubs of Alberta and Montana. It lives up to its designation in every way — though the country is wild, there are few more peaceful places on the United States-Canadian border. The Victorian-style Prince of Wales Hotel has an undeniably international flavor. The hotel is nestled among mountain peaks at the head of Waterton Lake, which extends more than seven miles (11 km) into Glacier National Park.

RIGHT:
Minerva Terrace, part of Mammoth Hot Springs, is composed of travertine, a form of calcium carbonate that has been dissolved from underground limestone and carried to the surface by hot water. The colors on the terraces are caused by bacteria and algae that find the hot springs a perfect place to live. Mammoth is near the north entrance of the park, and is its headquarters. From the time the park was established until 1918 when Park Service Rangers took on the job, army troops were stationed here to protect animals and tourists from each other.

RIGHT:

Morning Glory Pool is one of dozens of deep green-and-blue hot water springs in Yellowstone's thermal areas. The brilliant colors are caused by algae. The pools, paint pots, geysers, and steam vents are fed by underground volcanic activity that superheats the water table. In many places, the earth's crust is too fragile to support anything heavier than a fieldmouse, and the Park Service has built boardwalks that allow visitors to look.

∞

OPPOSITE PAGE:

A boardwalk runs across the thin crust of the West Thumb Geyser Basin for close-up views of the colorful hot springs. Water from rain and snow seeps into the ground, is heated either by the earth's magma or underground lava, and reemerges on the surface, either as a geyser or a mineral-rich pool of steaming hot water. It is an incredible sight at any time of the year, but especially impressive in the depths of winter, when the steam meets the air in what is often the coldest spot in the Continental United States.

RIGHT:

The Yellowstone River has cut this twenty-four mile- (39-km-) long, 1,200- foot- (366-m-) deep canyon through lava. The river cascades into the canyon in a pair of roaring waterfalls, one of which is twice as high as Niagara Falls. The park is one of the world's great wildlife refuges, but visitors looking down into the canyon are usually charmed by begging chipmunks who have known for generations that the scenery here generally turns a person into a soft touch.

© Travelpix/FPG International

California (1890)
1,189 square miles
(3,079 square kilometers)

YOSEMITE

LEFT:
The granite domes that protected the Yosemite Valley from the outside world for millions of years became a wonder to behold for men who had gone to California to find gold—and in the process found a priceless gift of nature. But as often happens, they began to think of ways to turn a profit on it. Fortunately, John Muir and others fought to protect it; but it was a slow process. It took nearly thirty years for them to convince the government to make the area off-limits to developers and another sixteen years to have the Yosemite Valley included in the preserve. In 1913, the Hech Hetchy Valley, which Muir said was "holy ground," was flooded to create a reservoir and part of the original park was lost forever.

RIGHT:

The combined height of the Upper and Lower Yosemite Falls and the Cascades between them is 2,425 feet (739 m), making this the third-highest waterfall in the world. All by itself, the Upper Fall is the world's seventh-highest, but Yosemite's Ribbon Fall is nearly 200 feet (61 m) higher. In fact, Yosemite has eight of the forty highest waterfalls in the world. The best time to see them in all their glory is the middle of May when snowmelt is at its peak. Sometimes in late summer the smaller waterfalls virtually disappear.

∞

OPPOSITE PAGE:

Half Dome is a testament to the power of the glacier that created the U-shaped valley, and an unusual feature of the skyline view from Yosemite Lodge. It was one of the landmarks John Muir had in mind when he wrote, "Of all the visitors to Yosemite, clouds are the most imposing . . . .

They seem to wedge and scramble among the roughest crags and swim and glide and drift down the canyons over smooth brows and sheer cliffs with peculiarly impressive gestures. And when a storm is breaking up, the light effects are marvelously effective and the whole grand show seems to be taking place in a walled room."

RIGHT:

The 317-foot (97-m) Vernal Fall is at the easternmost end of the Yosemite Valley, an area accessible only by shuttlebus or bicycle or, of course, on foot. It is reached by a steep trail a little more than a mile long, but the trip is well-worth the effort. More than 2.5 million people visit Yosemite every year, which makes it a good idea to get off the beaten path and explore the park's hidden corners. Along with the 594-foot (181-m) Nevada Fall nearby, Vernal marks the start of the John Muir Trail, named for the great naturalist who first saw the Sierra Nevada Mountains in 1868. His newspaper and magazine articles about Yosemite began the movement to make it America's second national park.

Utah (1919)
148 square miles
(383 square kilometers)

ZION

PREVIOUS PAGE:
The dramatic cliffs of Zion are made of Navajo sandstone, 2,200 feet (670 m) thick in some places. It was created some 150 million years ago by windblown sand that covered lakes, streams, and forests where dinosaurs once roamed. The forces that created it are still at work changing the landscape, and patches of blue that may not have been exposed even a few hundred years ago replace similar patches of red and yellow, as chunks of sandstone are worn away.

ABOVE:
Mountains in Zion have such names as "The Patriarchs," and several are designated as "temples." This one, called Lady Mountain, overlooks the Virgin River and is one of the highlights of the Zion Canyon Scenic Drive, a six-mile (10-km) dead end road leading to the spectacular Temple of the Sinawava. The canyon is still being formed by the Virgin River, which rushes through drops of more than 80 feet per mile (15 m/km) on its way to Lake Mead, 200 miles (322 km) to the southwest.

RIGHT:
The early Mormon settlers scratched out a living from farms in these rocky canyons and though their lives were hard, Isaac Bethunin saw nothing but beauty here. "These great mountains are the natural temples of God," he said. "We can worship here as well as in the man-made temples in Zion, the biblical 'Heavenly City of God.' Let us call it Little Zion." His neighbors were convinced that they could see the face of a watchman in the 6,555-foot (1,998-m) summit of this mountain and named it "The Watchman." It watches over the south entrance of the park.

INDEX